Decodable Reader
Unit 2

Contents

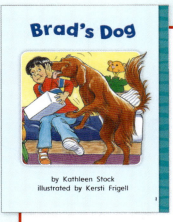

Brad's Dog 1
r-blends, *s*-blends

What Can I Get? 9
Short *e (e, ea)*

Big Bud 17
Short *u*

Camping Fun 25
End Blends *nd, nk, nt, st*

Trish Wants a Ship 33
Digraphs *th, sh, -ng*

Brad's Dog

by Kathleen Stock
illustrated by Kersti Frigell

Brad can sit.
Brad can jot.

Stan can **jump** on Brad.

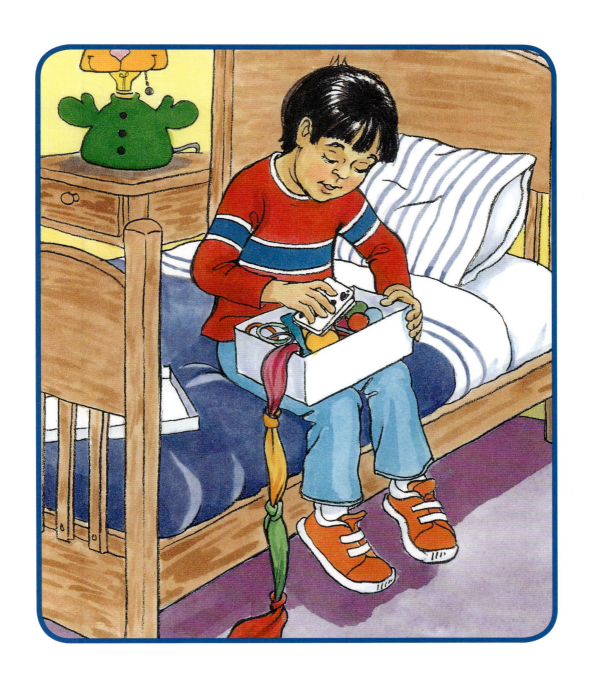

Brad can pick **two** tricks.

Stan licks. Brad grins.
Brad will **move** with Stan.

Brad and Stan **run**.
Brad trips.

Brad grabs Stan.
Stan is a pal.

What Can I Get?

by Isabel Johnson

I head in to a **new** spot.
What can I get here?

I can get bread.
It smells good!

I can get eggs.
There are six eggs in a box.

I can get red jam.
It is in a glass pot.

I will get **help** to pack up.
I will **use** a big tan bag.

I like this spot.
I will head back **again**.

Big Bud

by Vanessa Parks
illustrated by Louise Gardner

Big Bud is my dog.

I **live** with Big Bud.
Big Bud likes my rug.

Big Bud is a fun pup.

Big Bud runs.
Then he hops in mud!

I fill up a tub.
I smell suds!

One, two, **three**!
Big Bud gets in!

Could I hug Big Bud?
Yes!

Camping Fun

by Jamie Cydzik
illustrated by Sarah Dillard

Frank and Meg like camping!
Mom and Dad set up a tent.

Frank and Meg sit on a stump by plants.
Frank cast it in the pond.

No! A gust **of** wind!
Look at the mast slump.
It will sink **under**!

Who can mend it?
Mom can send it back.

Frank can bask in the Sun and **eat**.
Meg can jump in. Plunk!

This trip was just the best. Frank and Meg must come back!

Trish Wants a Ship

by Amisha Gray
illustrated by Jan Pyk

Trish picks up thin shells.
Trish can fish with a rod.

On this **day**, Trish has a wish.
"I **want** a good ship."

Trish spots a little ship.
It is stashed in Mom's shed.

Will Trish want this ship?
Trish can brush the dust.

Trish calls it Shellfish.
"All hands on deck!"

Zing! Trish taps a button.
Then Shellfish moves on.

Unit 2

Week 1 • *Brad's Dog* .... page 1
Word Count: 40

Decodable Words
Target Phonics Elements: *r*-Blends, *s*-Blends
Brad, grabs, grins, Stan, tricks, trips
Review: a, can, dog, is, jot, licks, on, pal, pick, sit, will

High-Frequency Words
jump, move, run, two
Review: and, with

Week 2 • *What Can I Get?* .... page 9
Word Count: 69

Decodable Words
Target Phonics Element: Short *e* (e, ea)
bread, eggs, get, head, red, smells
Review: a, back, bag, big, box, can, glass, in, is, it, jam, pack, pot, six, spot, tan, will

High-Frequency Words
again, help, new, there, use
Review: are, good, here, I, like, the, this, to, up, what

Week 3 • *Big Bud* .... page 17
Word Count: 53

Decodable Words
Target Phonics Element: Short *u*
Bud, fun, hug, mud, pup, rug, runs, suds, tub, up
Review: *a, big, dog, fill, gets, had, him, hops, in, is, smell*

High-Frequency Words
could, live, one, then, three
Review: *do, he, I, likes, my, the, to, two, what, with*

Week 4 • *Camping Fun* .... page 25
Word Count: 72

Decodable Words
Target Phonics Elements: End Blends *nd, nk, nt, st*
and, bask, best, Frank, gust, just, mast, mend, must, plant, plunk, pond, send, sink, tent, wind
Review: *a, at, back, camping, can, Dad, in, it, jump, Meg, Mom, on, set, sit, trip, up, will*

High-Frequency Words
eat, of, no, under, who
Review: *by, come, like, look, the*

Week 5 • *Trish Wants a Ship*............ page 33
Word Count: 65

Decodable Words
Target Phonics Elements: Consonant Digraphs: *th, sh, -ng*
brush, fish, shed, Shellfish, shells, ship, stashed, then, thin, this, Trish, wish, with, zing
Review: *a, button, can, deck, dust, hands, has, in, Mom's, on, picks, rod, spots, taps, up, will*

High-Frequency Words
all, call, day, her, want
Review: *good, little, moves, the*

Decoding skills taught to date:

Phonics: Short *a*; Short *i*; *l*-Blends; Short *o*; *r*-Blends, *s*-Blends; Short *e* (*e, ea*); Short *u*; End Blends *nd, nk, nt, st, sk, mp*; Consonant Digraphs: *th, sh, -ng*

Structural Analysis: Inflectional Ending -*s* (plurals, verbs); Double Final Consonants; Alphabetical Order; Possessives with *'s*; Inflectional Ending -*ed*; Contractions with *'s*; Inflectional Ending -*ing*; Closed Syllables